Buess, Bob.
Deliverance from the bondage of fear : ref. 2 Timothy 1:7

DELIVERANCE FROM THE BONDAGE OF FEAR

ref. 2 Timothy 1:7

by Bob Buess

DELIVERANCE
FROM THE BONDAGE OF FEAR
by Bob Buess

Order Books From
Bob Buess
Box 959
Van, Texas 75790

Price: $1.50

Send 60¢ postage for the first three books ordered by mail.

Add 5¢ for each additional book.

Texas residents include 4% sales tax.

Individuals may deduct a 35% discount in orders of 30 books or more. Texas residents please include sales tax after the discount is figured.

CONTENTS

INTRODUCTION

Fear is a monster, but it is never to be feared by a believer in Jesus Christ.

Christ is in every believer. He is the champion of all who believe. None is greater than our Lord Jesus Christ.

If you are not absolutely sure that Jesus Christ dwells in your heart, pray this prayer with me; and mean it with all your heart:

Lord Jesus, I am a sinner. I believe that you died for me on the cross. I believe you paid my sin debt. I now yield my all to you. The best I know how, I surrender to you. Right now, I accept you as my Lord and Saviour.

Now regardless of feeling begin to consider it so. You are a child of God. You are a new creature. Start acting like a member of the heavenly kingdom.

The new birth itself is one of the most powerful weapons that we have. In the new birth, we receive the life of Christ Jesus. We receive His nature. Fear is the devil's nature. God does not give us the spirit of fear, but of power and of love and of a sound mind. 2 Timothy 1:7. Since fear is the enemy's nature, you can renounce it and live in your Father's nature which is love, joy, and a sound mind.

1 Corinthians 3:21. "All things are yours." You now reign in this life by Jesus Christ. Romans 5:17. All things are now under your feet. Luke 10:19. Now stand firm in this new position in Jesus Christ.

Rejoice in the presence of problems. They only give God an opportunity to show Himself strong on your behalf. As you rejoice, your problems will soon disappear.

> Jeremiah 42:11 "Be not afraid of the king of Babylon of whom ye are afraid; be not afraid of him . . . I am with you to save you, and to deliver you from his hand."

Satan would have you look at the circumstances and become alarmed. God would have you look to Him and rest in His finished work for you.

Do not fear the king of Babylon. For you, that may be fear itself. It may be problems in the home. It may be financial problems. It may be problems in the community or government. Fear will soon destroy those who entertain it.

Colossians 2:15 teaches that Satan and his power has been dstroyed. You can stop identifying with fear. It is not your nature. You may still feel fearful, but do not go by feelings. Resist the devil, and he will flee from you.

Identify with your new nature. Romans 6:11. Consider yourself dead to sin and alive unto God. Fear may still be present. Laugh at it. True, you might not feel like laughing because it has a strong hold on you. Just keep on laughing at it. Keep on identifying with your new Christ nature. You do not legally possess fear. It is an intrusion from the enemy. He must go. He is getting weaker. Keep on believing. He will soon leave.

If you are so completely controlled by the spirit of fear that you feel helpless, then contact a Christian brother who understands deliverance; and get further help.

Fear brings sickness, failure, turmoil, con fusion, frustrations, and finally, prematur death.

CHAPTER I

THE SOURCE OF FEAR

Fear is the nature of the devil. 2 Timothy 1:7. "God has not given us the spirit of fear . . . " Regardless of the particular problem, fear comes from the devil.

Fear can come from many directions. We will not go into all of these here. We will discuss a few to get your thinking and understanding flowing together so that you may relate to these.

OVER CORRECTION IN CHILDHOOD

Ephesians 6:4 "Ye fathers, provoke not your children to wrath: but bring them up in the nurture and admonition of the Lord."

Abuse by parents brings many adverse reactions in the emotional and mental makeup of a child which carry over into adult years.

Children who have been abused by a parent or teacher by extreme correction delivered in the spirit of anger tend to be fearful and timid.

These children may react in different ways. Some withdraw into a shell of insecurity and fear; others enter into rebellion against all forms of authority.

One lad reverted to violence. When I cast out this spirit, the devil began to cry out, "Stop pushing me around. You aren't going to push me around." He left. The lad was free from rebellion and fear.

One teen-age girl had been dominated by an unwise father and a mentally sick school teacher who kept calling her abusive names such as: "You stupid, ignorant brat." As this girl would enter into groups, fear would so dominate her thinking that she would feel like crawling under the table or getting alone by herself.

Thank the Lord, she, too, received a glorious deliverance.

ACCIDENTS OF VARIOUS TYPES CAN CREATE FEAR

One pastor's wife who had been in an automobile accident was dominated by fear. It would hit her every time she would get into a car. Upon deliverance from this, she was perfectly normal.

ABNORMAL ATTITUDES AMONG PARENTS

Parental fighting in front of the children creates emotional disturbances which allow or cause them to have insecurity, fear, or mental blocks.

A parent who is alcoholic creates such an instability in a child that, in many cases, this carries over to adult life.

ABNORMAL MARRIED LIFE CREATES FEAR

Fighting and turmoil in a married couple can cause a violent reaction within the emotional life of one or both partners. A strong domineering husband who has little consideration for his partner can cause the wife to react by withdrawing into a dream world or by assuming violent, defensive attitudes. She later may succomb to self pity, suicide, etc. Fear of living, fear of men, or fear of every moment of life may begin to take the dominant roll of her thinking.

When one partner learns that the other is running around with another person in an unfaithful manner, fear and insecurity sometimes come to them.

This partner has a choice. He or she can move above it and live victoriously or yield to fears, self-condemnation, self-pity, or a multiple of similar attitudes.

BUSINESS REVERSES CAN CREATE FEAR

The 1929 stock market crash is a good example here. Men in fear and desperation took their lives in no small number.

SIN AND REBELLION AGAINST GOD BRING FEAR

One lady recently said that before she and her husband were saved, she became pregnant. Her husband became angry; heated arguments followed which lasted for days. The wife became so confused and frustrated that she lost the baby. Later, she developed such a fear of having a child, that when she finally wanted children, she could not carry a child over a few weeks.

We had the privilege of seeing her delivered from this spirit of fear in Jesus' name.

One girl had lived with crime and violence all of her life. Her family had several criminals in it. She was involved in sex abuse. By the time I saw her, she was tormented with fear, nervousness, and suicidal tendencies. She was delivered in Jesus' name.

THE ATTITUDE OF FEAR CAN BE TRANSMITTED TO OTHERS

A mother or father full of fear can transmit this to the children. Much of the fear problem that I deal with comes from parental fear. The child is thoroughly indoctrinated with these attitudes during childhood. When adulthood comes, his heart is a perfect seedbed for Satan.

Just recently a mother and daughter came to me for help. The mother was full of fear, frustration, hate, etc. The child had a mental block and had not developed beyond her early teens. She was twice that age at the time. Parental discord due to fighting and infidelity created fear of adulthood.

Fear within the executives of a business can be transmitted to the employees to the extent that the business will fail.

Fear within a nation can be transmitted to such an extent that it invades the entire framework of the society. This allows them to fall to smaller nations. Gideon told all the fearful ones to go home. Over and over God's Word tells us not to fear the enemy. God knows fear will grow and be transmitted to others. Fear is like a seed. Sow it in your heart, and it will grow more of like seed.

CHAPTER 2

THE RESULTS OF FEAR

FEAR BRINGS SICKNESS

Proverbs 15:13 "A merry heart maketh a cheerful countenance: but by sorrow of the heart the spirit is broken."

Proverbs 17:22 "A merry heart doeth good like a medicine: but a broken spirit drieth the bones."

Doctors are finding that heart attacks, ulcers, etc. are triggered by fear and anxiety more than any other cause.

A merry heart is like a medicine. A broken spirit drieth the bones. In the marrow of the bone is where the blood is manufactured. A broken, fearful spirit is probably responsible for more cancer and heart trouble than the better known killers.

FEAR BRINGS BONDAGE

Proverbs 29:25 "The fear of man bringeth a snare: but whoso putteth his trust in the Lord shall be safe."

Job 3:25 "The thing which I greatly feared is come upon me."

Fear of man, whether it be your boss, employees, husband, wife, or competition in the business world, will bring nothing but snares.

"The thing I greatly feared is come." Perhaps this was Job's real problem. If there is a great fear deep down inside, deal with it now. It will soon come out and be your "waterloo."

Some folks observe trends in their family line, such as the history of sickness in close relatives, and then draw the conclusion that they will get the same infirmities. Fear soon begins to grip them until they are paralyzed, and in many cases, they actually begin to develop the same symptoms.

Recently a lady came to us completely dominated by fear due to constantly reminding herself of the cancer and other infirmities in the female organs of her mother and sisters. Fear so completely controlled her that she was afraid to have children of her own.

We cast this spirit out in Jesus' name. She

screamed and screamed as it came out. What a glorious deliverance and rejoicing the Lord gave this girl. All fear to have children completely left her.

If there is any area of your life that has been invaded by fear, even though it be slight now, deal with it or it will soon grow and develop into a monster that will bring sickness, premature death, or other problems.

The best way to deal with fear will be by rejoicing in the Lord and confessing aloud several times a day: "I am free. Jesus has set me free. I will not have any bondages." You may name the problem you fear such as sickness, failure, poverty, accident, etc.

FEAR BRINGS TORMENTS

One lady had been to a fortune teller (seance or witch), and she, later, kept hearing steps in her house at night. She went to another witch to get the curse removed. As a result of this visit, she picked up more demons. They would come and torture her at night. She felt like they were injecting needles into her arms at night.

This woman lived in constant hell on earth. After she was delivered in Jesus' name, she looked twenty years younger.

FEAR BRINGS FAILURE

Judges 7:3 "Whosoever is fearful and afraid, let him return and depart early from mount Gilead."

Gideon knew the power of fear. He would be better off with a handful without fear than a multitude of cowards.

Fear is like a short circuit. It destroys the real power.

Twenty two thousand left Gideon because of fear. Later all but three hundred left. With three hundred who had no fear, God was able to bring victory.

Fear is a failure spirit sent from hell to destroy you. Do not entertain it or allow it to stay with you. Rejoice your way to victory in the face of all problems.

Isaiah 37:6-7 " . . . Be not afraid of the words that thou hast heard, wherewith the servants of the king of Assyria have blasphemed . . . behold, I will send a blast upon him . . . I will cause him to fall by the sword in his own land."

Jeremiah 1:8 "Be not afraid of their faces: for I am with thee to deliver thee, saith the Lord."

Exodus 14:13 "Fear ye not, stand still,

and see the salvation of the Lord . . .”

Psalm 91:5 “Thou shalt not be afraid for the terror by night; nor for the arrow that flieth by day.”

Deuteronomy 20:1, 3 “When thou goest out to battle against thine enemies, and seest horses, and chariots, and a people more than thou, be not afraid of them: for the Lord thy God is with thee . . . Fear not, and do not tremble, neither be ye terrified because of them.”

2 Chronicles 20:15 “ . . . Be not afraid nor dismayed by reason of this great multitude; for the battle is not yours, but God's.”

These are just a few of the scriptures exhorting you on the danger of fear. God's power is at your disposal. You can yield to joy and faith at any moment and enjoy the victory, or you can yield to fear and see Satan make havoc out of your life.

“Be not afraid of their words.” Satan would have you believe his lies or his symptoms. Yielding to this will destroy you. Refuse to go by your feelings or sight. Laugh at yourself and go on.

“Be not afraid of their faces.” The enemy may look terrible. He may look powerful. The enemy's face to you may be sickness. Fear ye not. It may be problems on the job. Fear ye not. It may be family problems. Fear ye not. Learn to rejoice your way through your situations.

"Fear ye not, stand still." The flesh likes to get you involved in fear, nervousness, and struggle. Stand still, and rejoice in the Lord. This gets fear and self out of the picture; then the Lord steps forward and blesses you with great victories. This is true faith. Faith is a rest. Fear is a constant struggle.

"When thou goest out to battle against thine enemies, and seest horses, and chariots, and a people more than thou, be not afraid of them." No problem is greater in power than the Lord thy God. He is with you. He will never forsake you. Do not look at your problem, or it will create fear and generate more problems. Your enemy may be ten times larger than you; he may be a thousand times larger than you; but in Jesus' name, you are never under. You can do all things through Christ who strengtheneth you. You are never under any problem. Keep your eyes on Jesus.

One missionary was sick unto death. The doctors gave him up. The Lord appeared to him and said, "If you will keep fear out of your spirit, then I can heal you." From that moment on, he refused to yield to fear. God healed him.

Every time the children of God faced a

problem, the Lord always said, "Fear ye not."

FEAR CAN BRING DEATH

I recently read about a group of seniors initiating an underclassman. They tied him to the railroad tracks and then left him. He could hear the train coming in the distance. He did not know that he was on a siding. When the boys returned to get him, they found that he was dead. Fear had so taken hold of him that it gave him heart failure.

It is also reported by many that most of the snake bite victims die from fear rather than the venom.

CHAPTER 3

HOW TO OVERCOME FEAR

FEAR IS OVERCOME BY ABIDING IN THE TRUTH OF GOD

John 8:32 "And ye shall know the truth, and the truth shall make you free."

John 15:7 "If ye abide in me, and my words abide in you, ye shall ask what ye will, and it shall be done unto you."

I have seen people set free from the demons of fear by confessing simple truths from the Word of God. God's Word is spirit. John 6:63. God's Word will cut like a sword. Hebrews 4:12. There is nothing more powerful than the Word of God.

As you abide in the Word, freedom from fear develops and brings you into full control of every situation.

Symptoms may declare that fear is coming

back. Start singing and rejoicing and worshipping the Lord. Fear cannot stand a victory spirit rooted and grounded in the Word of God. Fear will leave when the truth reaches your spirit

> **Psalm 112:7-8 "He shall not be afraid of evil tidings: his heart is fixed, trusting in the Lord. His heart is established, he shall not be afraid . . ."**

Learning to overcome fear before it gets hold of you is most effective. This is, by far, the best way to deal with fear.

The time to resist an attack is at the beginning. You would be foolish to wait until the attacker overcame you. Likewise, in the spiritual battle, the time to resist fear or other related attitudes or spirits is at the beginning of the attack. To wait a few hours, days, or weeks merely allows the enemy to overpower you.

Stand on the Word of God the moment a problem arises. Do not react carnally with worry, frustration, fear, confusion, or other sinful attitudes. Let God be true and every experience a lie. Stand on what the Word of God says. Experience and fact may declare that you are going under. Ignore this. The Word says, "If you have faith, nothing shall be impossible unto you." Matthew 17:20. "I can do all things through Christ which strengthens me." Philippians 4:13.

I am more than a conqueror through Him that loved me. Romans 8:37.

Get a promise that meets your situation. Stand on it. Sing praises to the Lord using this promise as a basis. Rejoice!

The Word of God has now built a shield around you. Fear cannot enter.

> **Psalm 91:4 "... His truth shall be thy shield and buckler."**

> **Proverbs 15:4 "A wholesome tongue is a tree of life: but perverseness therein a breach in the spirit."**

As you confess God's spirit Word, it becomes a protective shield warding off the enemy. Your tongue creates life around you. You can speak victory into being. Through Jesus and His living Word you become creative. Your tongue becomes a tree of life. On the other hand, as you yield to circumstances and fear, then you become a victim of the enemy. Your tongue becomes a breach in your spirit protection. Your shield is broken by negative attitudes. You open the door of your life to the intrusion of the enemy.

"He shall not be afraid of evil tidings." This man is grounded in the Word. He is a man of faith. He is a man fully "trusting in the Lord." He is in his rest.

Allow your spirit to be upset and fearful, and you allow the enemy to invade your life.

Develop a victory spirit by daily confessing the Word of God. You will soon come to the place that symptoms, alarms, and pressures do not throw you off course.

> 2 Samuel 22:33-35 "God is my strength and power: and he maketh my way perfect. He maketh my feet like hinds' feet: and setteth me upon my high places. He teacheth my hands to war; so that a bow of steel is broken by mine arms."

Agree with God's Word. Disregard your present condition of fear and frustration. Treat the Word of God as though God spoke it to you directly. It may not come through strongly at first, but hold on until the truth routs the enemy. Allow yourself to become rooted with victorious attitudes in your spirit.

Agree with the Word. "God is my strength and power." Say it over and over. Believe the Word rather than the lie of the enemy. Fear is not your nature. It is a lie. It is an invasion from Satan. He has no legal right in you. Stop agreeing with him.

"He maketh my way perfect." Believe this. Meditate on it. Let this become a way of life with you. You have believed fear and the things that have created fear in your life for many years. Now give God a fair chance to show himself strong. Confess over and over: "He maketh my way perfect. He maketh my feet like hinds' feet. He setteth me upon my high places." Refuse what you see and feel. The Word of God will soon begin to take root in you and form your basic thinking.

Never allow yourself to think fearful, negative thoughts of failure. These are demonic. Encourage yourself at all times with the Word of God.

Confess boldly, regardless of feelings and present thought pattern: "He teacheth my hands to war; so that a bow of steel is broken by mine arms." I am a victor today. Jesus is with me today. I am strong today. I have favor with God and man today. My life is useful. God has His hand on me. He is working things out.

Now take time to worship and love the Lord Jesus. Let your spirit reach out to Him through these truths in the spirit of worship. Allow your spirit to bathe in the heavenly presence of our Lord.

You were born to be an overcomer. Your feet are like hinds' feet. You can jump over any barrier that the enemy may erect in your path. You are a soldier with all the latest spirit equipment necessary to destroy the enemy. "A bow of steel is broken by mine arms."

Satan has been handing you a "bill of goods." Renounce it. Refuse to be fenced in.

You can jump over all your problems and land in the arms of Jesus, free indeed. "If the Son therefore shall make you free, ye shall be free indeed." John 8:36.

STRONG CONFIDENCE DESTROYS FEAR

Isaiah 30:15 "In returning and rest shall ye be saved; in quietness and in confidence shall be your strength . . ."

Exodus 14:13-14 "Fear ye not, stand still, and see the salvation of the Lord, which he will shew to you today: for the Egyptians whom ye have seen today, ye shall see them again no more for ever. The Lord shall fight for you, and ye shall hold your peace."

Psalm 56:11 "In God have I put my trust: I will not be afraid what man can do unto me."

Proverbs 14:26 "In the fear of the Lord is strong confidence; and his children shall have a place of refuge."

Hebrews 10:35-36 "Cast not away therefore your confidence which hath great recompense of reward. Ye have need of patience, that, after ye have done the will of God, ye might receive the promise."

"In quietness and in confidence shall be your strength." This is the restful spirit. Learn to get quiet in the face of your problems and relax. Fear feeds on anxiety, strife, turmoil, and confusion. Develop the quiet and confident spirit. God has all the answers worked out. Turn to Him in confidence. Watch Him bring you through your "Red Sea" experience.

"Fear ye not, stand still, and see." Refuse to push the panic button. Stand still. Relax. Confess the Word. Rejoice. Laugh at your problem. Don't let Satan push you around. Refuse to yield to the fleshly activities of worry and fear.

You are now in a position to see the salvation of God.

Soon you will see your enemy no more. He will drown in the flood of your deliverance.

"I will not be afraid what man can do." Fear of man will bring a snare. Your deliverance is not based on your spiritual ability to overpower your enemy. It is not based on your mental ability. It is not based on your personality. It is not even based on your good works. Your deliverance from fear is based on releasing the power of Jesus Christ.

Spiritual achievements, mental abilities, strong personalities, etc. are definite factors in deliverance from fear and maintaining such deliverance. They are blessings from the Lord. These are not to be minimized. These work together like faith and works. Works are important, but they are useless without faith.

"In God have I put my trust." This being so, relax; get out of the struggle. It is the Lord's battle not yours. If you insist on doing it yourself, your fears will grow; and your problem will get worse.

This might be described as the reckless, carefree faith. Commit it to the Lord, and go on your way in your wonderful confidence in your wonderful Saviour.

"In the fear of the Lord is strong confidence." This would require an entire book to cover completely, but it has to do with reverence to Him and obedience to His Word. As we do this, we have a strong refuge in the Lord.

"Cast not away therefore your confidence . . . ye have need of patience . . ." You have taken a step of faith. Cast not away your confidence. The seed you planted is now in the process of taking root. Give it a fair chance to bring forth results in your life.

A complexity of problems sometimes takes deep root in an individual.

Sometimes these problems involve other people and their wills.

The Lord is gentle. He is longsuffering. He does not force.

Have patience. Relax. God will bring you through on a red carpet in due time. You will soon receive the promise.

Confidence is based on Jesus Christ in you. You may as well admit that you can do all things through Christ. Philippians 4:13. You are more than a conqueror today. Romans 8:37. Nothing is impossible. Matthew 17:20.

FEAR IS OVERCOME BY GIVING THANKS

Psalm 106:47 "Save us, O Lord our God, and gather us from among the heathen, to give thanks unto thy holy name, and to triumph in thy praise."

2 Chronicles 20:22 "When they began to sing and to praise, the Lord set ambushments against the children of Ammon, Moab, and Mount Seir, which were come against Judah; and they were smitten."

Acts 16:25 "At midnight Paul and Silas prayed and sang praises unto God: and the prisoners heard them."

Ephesians 5:20 "Giving thanks always for all things unto God and the Father in the name of our Lord Jesus Christ."

I Thessalonians 5:18 "In every thing give thanks; for this is the will of God in Christ Jesus concerning you."

Romans 8:28 "And we know that all things work together for good to them that love God . . ."

"To triumph in thy praise." Jericho's walls came down when the people praised God. Paul and Silas praised God in prison at midnight, and the Lord sent an earthquake and set them free.

Victory comes when you yield to a victory spirit.

Failure comes when you yield to a failure spirit.

Take your choice.

"At midnight Paul and Silas prayed and sang praises unto God." Instead of grumbling, fussing, complaining, and worrying about being in jail, they rejoiced and worshipped the Lord.

"And suddenly there was a great earthquake . . . all the doors were opened, and every one's bands were loosed." Acts 16:26. Things happen smoothly when we praise and worship the Lord regardless of feeling and circumstance.

Recently I heard of a missionary in Mexico who had been put in jail. He "groaned and moaned." He fussed at God for getting him in such a mess. He developed a persecution complex. Finally, the Lord spoke to him: "I will never leave thee." From then on, the Lord became so real that he felt in His presence at all times. During the remainder of his stay in jail he said, "I experienced absolute freedom in the presence of bondage." Immediately after his attitude changed, they brought him food and water. He hadn't had either for two days prior to this. The following day he was released.

"When they began to sing and to praise, the Lord set ambushments against the children of Ammon . . ." Trouble and lots of it was the order of the day for God's children. Satan was giving the orders until the children of the Lord interrupted his plans by prayer, fasting, and praise. Hallelujah. You do not have to submit to Satan's blueprint for your life.

They prepared themselves for action by prayer and fasting. At the edge of the battle front they decided to praise the Lord. They got caught up in the spirit of praise which probably lasted from three to six hours. When the spirit of praise lifted, they discovered that the Lord had destroyed the enemy for them.

Your enemy, too, can be destroyed by seeking the Lord and offering up a praise from the depths of your soul in an audible voice.

"Giving thanks always for all things unto God." This is faith's way of meeting the problem. Most of you are geared to "grumbling and complaining" in the face of problems. Fear enters and causes you to panic.

In the face of problems, the only way to

get the victory is to rejoice and say, "Thank you, Father. You are still my God, and I know you will work it out."

"In every thing give thanks; for this is the will of God." Yes, regardless of your problem and fear, do not accept it as a permanent fixture. Laugh at it. Laugh at yourself. Relax. Look up to Jesus, and say, "Thank you, Lord. You are a wonderful Savior. You can handle this one, too."

Now you have entered true rest. Regardless of your problem, rest in Jesus.

We were having a seminar in Yuma, Arizona, recently. As we arrived, we found that the management of the motel had "goofed." They had scheduled another meeting for the same room and at the same hour we were to meet. When we entered and saw the other group, I smiled and said, "Thank you, Lord." My wife said, "Well, lets see how He works this one out."

Well, He worked it out. He, through the management, had scheduled another room in another motel nearby. As our people would arrive, the receptionist would detour them over to the other motel. This night was one of the best meetings of the entire week.

Progress in the kingdom of God has been blocked many times by the devil of fear.

Many tests come just before promotion.

The only way to get a passing grade in the faith walk is by praising the Lord in the face of apparent failure and defeat.

By giving thanks for all things regardless of feeling or emotion, we operate in a strong positive faith.

Satan cannot operate in this atmosphere. The atmosphere in which he works best is negative. Fear is strongly negative.

To give thanks in the face of all problems is to insult the devil. This causes him to throw his forces in reverse and leave. He cannot stand a strong Jesus atmosphere.

"All things work together for good . . ." God is able to take every mistake, every failure, and every attack from the enemy and turn it to His glory.

Satan means to hurt you.

God wants to take that effort of Satan and turn it into a blessing for you.

The next time trouble strikes, laugh at it; and thank the Lord. Blessings from heaven will begin to flow to you immediately.

The first impulse to any problem from the carnal man is to fear. The carnal man, when faced with a problem, too often begins to cry out: "Get a doctor, get a preacher, get a counselor, Oh, I wonder if I can get my faith working." Or he may be so far down that he gives up completely.

Have a laugh at the next problem, pain, or apparent failure. Have a "ball" the next time trouble comes. God is "fixing" to bless you. This is just a small "Red Sea" before crossing over to a greater place of victory.

Do not fail your test.

Slip your hands up; and worship and thank the Lord. He is doing a work of perfecting and purging in you. Get excited. Be thankful before the Lord. Worship and love Him.

If you have sinned, quickly repent. Move back into a right relationship with the Lord.

Refuse the spirit of self-condemnation. It will drain and defeat you. God has forgiven you. Forgive yourself, and get happy.

Arise above your problems of failure, frustrations, and confusions by "joying" and rejoicing in the Lord.

Just recently, I counseled a minister over the phone. This person was very depressed. Bills were coming in; and very little money was available to pay them. Persecutions and misunderstandings were involved, too. I showed this minister what I have been showing you. I advised him to rejoice and "joy."

In fact, I told him just to say "joy" every time he thought about or was faced with a problem.

I received a call the next day. It was a different person on the phone. Instead of being defeated and despondent, this same minister was rejoicing and saying: "Joy, joy, joy." Victory had completely routed the enemy.

Many fail to move to new ministries or new levels in the faith walk because they accept failure and fear.

Move beyond your present faith level to new glories and faith by looking unto Jesus. 2 Corinthians 3:18. We are to go from glory to glory. Romans 1:17. We are to go from faith to faith.

Looking to self, confusion, sorrows, and disappointments brings you lower and lower. Looking unto Jesus and His life will bring you higher and higher.

We can only move on by "joying" in the Lord.

Put your complete confidence in His ability.

JOY BRINGS DELIVERANCE FROM FEAR

> Nehemiah 8:10 "The joy of the Lord is your strength."

> Isaiah 12:3 "With joy shall ye draw water out of the wells of salvation."

> Proverbs 17:22 "A merry heart doeth good like a medicine: but a broken spirit drieth the bones."

Joy is the fruit of the spirit. Joy is God's nature. Identify with the joy spirit. Fear comes to naught in the atmosphere of joy.

As I move into a situation that normally would drain my victory, I begin to "joy in the Lord." Many times, I simply begin to repeat the word joy over and over. This takes my mind off the problem and turns me to Jesus and His way. Joy and victory follow immediately.

"The joy of the Lord is your strength." Joy is the stronger spirit. Fear is a weak spirit out of hell. Refuse it. Press the joy button. As you rejoice and "joy" in your daily walk, strength flows from God to you. This is a matter of learning to yield to the right spirit.

"With joy shall ye draw water out of the wells of salvation." If you want water out of an open well, you must draw it with a rope and bucket. If you want water of life from Jesus you draw it but not with a natural bucket; you draw from the well of deliverance with the rope and bucket called joy.

Go about your daily activities with the spirit of joy. Repeat over and over, "Joy, joy, joy." Continue to look to Jesus.

"A merry heart hath a continual feast." For years, many have been taught by circumstances to be negative, fearful, and sad in the face of unpleasant situations. For many, this spirit is well rooted and grounded within. This spirit must be overthrown. Constantly develop attitudes of joy and rejoicing. The merry heart nath a continual feast. He is filled with blessings.

"A merry heart doeth good like a medicine." Joy and rejoicing are healing for the body. Joy is healing for the spirit. It is healing for the home. It is healing for the nation.

"A broken spirit drieth the bones." A sad spirit will eventually destroy you. Pressures sometimes drive folks from joy, health, and victory to defeat, fear, sadness, and failure because they have not learned that "joy" is the stronger spirit. As you deliberately yield to joy, you are learning to overcome the spirit of fear and sadness which kills all of your victories.

Problems with your companion, children, employees, employer, health, or other things are no excuse for you to become depressed. Anyone that has Jesus has the beginning and the ending of every situation. They have the answer. Jesus is more powerful than any multiple of problems.

Your apparent problem is not really your problem. Your ignorance is your problem. When you learn to "joy" in the midst of strife, fear, and failure, you will arise above these to new heights and excitements in Jesus.

Constantly looking for a better home, better job, or better education will not bring victory.

The only thing that will bring victory for you is to "joy" in what you have. Expect a better situation at home and on the job, but learn to rejoice right now.

Joy will set you free.
Fear will bind you.
Joy is like a medicine.
Fear is a poison.

Deuteronomy 28:47-48 "Because thou servedst not the Lord thy God with joyfulness, and with gladness of heart, for the abundance of all things, therefore shalt thou serve thine enemies which the Lord shall send against thee . . ."

Learn to be content with such things as you have. A coveteous and restless spirit are sinful. Rejoice in your present situation. Do not accept unpleasant situations as permanent, but learn to rejoice and be content. A spirit of contentment does not mean that you cannot move on to greater blessings; it merely means you are in a rest. Jesus will help you to work it out.

Go home; and rejoice in your home, your partner, and your children. They could stand some improvements, but keep on rejoicing for your many blessings that you have right now.

Major on the good things God has given you. Do not major on the shortcomings of the wife, husband, or children. Do not major on your financial shortcomings.

Rejoice in the multitude of blessings that you have. Confess for greater victories at home, in the children, etc. They will soon come. Joy is the order of the day.

The scripture above says, "because you do not serve the Lord with joyfulness and gladness of heart, then you will serve your enemies in the want of all things." A grumbling, complaining spirit is detestable in the sight of God.

Get your eyes off the shortcomings about you, and get them on the goodness of the Lord. Develop that happy and joyful spirit. Herein is your deliverance.

Some wives get so depressed because of the shortcomings of their husbands that they soon yield to a negative, fearful, grumbling, complaining, bitter spirit. Their sin becomes worse than their husband's. This same is true on the part of the husband with a problem wife.

ACTIVE FAITH DESTROYS FEAR

> Isaiah 35:3-4 "Strengthen ye the weak hands, and confirm the feeble knees, say to them that are of a fearful heart, Be strong, fear not . . . God will come and save you."

Christ is in every believer. Ephesians 3:17.

You have received his fulness. John 1:16.

You have power and authority to release his works. John 14:12.

Satan is under your feet. Luke 10:19.

You are seated with Christ. Ephesians 2:6.

Therefore you can "Say to the fearful heart, Be strong, fear not . . ." This is active faith. Lift up your hands and repeat this quietly before the Lord. "I stand on the faith and power of Jesus Christ. I resist and renounce the spirit of fear. I am strong today in Jesus Christ."

John 8:32 unfolds to you that as you know the truth, then you are set free. You are made free from fear by standing tall and firm in the Word of God. Truth as revealed in the Word of God by the Holy Spirit sends the enemy on his way.

Refuse your feelings. They will lie to you. Walk by the Word of God.

Matthew 8:25-26 "His disciples came to him, and awoke him, saying, Lord, save us: we perish. And he said unto them, Why are ye fearful, O ye of little faith? Then he arose, and rebuked the winds and the sea; and there was a great calm."

Matthew 17:20 "If ye have faith . . . nothing shall be impossible to you."

Ephesians 3:12 "In whom we have boldness and access with confidence by the faith of him."

James 2:20 "Faith without works is dead."

Exodus 14:15-16 "And the Lord said unto Moses, wherefore criest thou unto me? Speak unto the children of Israel, that they go forward. But lift thou up thy rod, and stretch out thine hand over the sea, and divide it . . ."

2 King 4:3-4 "Go, borrow thee vessels abroad of all thy neighbours, even empty vessels; borrow not a few. And when thou art come in, thou shalt shut the door upon thee and upon thy sons, and shalt pour out into all those vessels, and thou shalt set aside that which is full."

"Why are ye fearful?" Circumstances demand that you fear. Jesus demands that you ignore the circumstances. A storm was about to destroy the disciples in the little boat. In their fear and distress, they awoke Jesus from His rest. He rebuked them for not using their faith. "Why are ye fearful?" was His question. The Lord expects something out of sons. You are His ambassadors. He expects you to have complete authority over all circumstances.

"He arose and rebuked the winds and the sea; and there was a great calm." May the true sons of power come forth in this very hour.

Do not disappoint the Lord any longer. Arise, ye sons of God; and come forth into strength. Fear ye not the circumstances. Let your problem be a challenge to bring forth the Christ that abides within.

As Jesus released His faith, a great calm followed. Faith demands an action on your part.

Refuse to yield to fear. Faith alone brings victory. Fear will only bring bondage. You have a choice to make. Make the right choice. Choose to be active in releasing your faith, today.

One sister recently testified in one of our services the following: "I was harassed and controlled by fears and frustrations. My life was a constant battleground. I would stand before the Lord and boldly declare: 'I choose to serve Jesus Christ. I will to serve Jesus Christ.' My faith would rise for a while. Peace would come. Then seemingly out of nowhere, fear and turmoil would return. Over and over I would firmly declare, 'I choose to serve the Lord. I choose to have peace. I choose to have peace. I refuse fear and frustrations.' Finally, after days of struggle and warfare, Jesus set me completely free. I am normal today.' "

Fight the good fight of faith. Lay hold on these eternal realities is the essence of I Timothy 6:12. Be strong in the Lord is the command of Ephesians 6:10. Rule in the midst of thy problem is the command of Psalms 110:2.

You shall rule over your oppressors and fears is the truth contained in Isaiah 14:2.

Refuse to yield to fear. Determine to fight the good fight of faith. Determine to lay hold on these eternal golden nuggets. Be strong in the power of Christ today. Rule right now in the midst of your problem. Rule over your situation.

Hallelujah. Jesus has made you a warrior with victory given in advance. He has already destroyed fear. Colossians 2:15. "Having spoiled principalities and powers." Release your faith, today. Join the ranks of the kings and priests of Revelation 1:6. ". . . Hath made us kings and priests unto God."

"Nothing shall be impossible with you." Christ is in you. You have His faith.

"We have boldness and access with confidence by the faith of him."

Satan lies destroyed at your feet. Refuse to give fear a place in your life. Arise and give the devil "a run for his money." Let him taste fear. He is afraid of you. Stop his bluff today. Nothing is impossible with you since Jesus Christ is in you. You have boldness and access to heaven's power by His faith. Get excited about Jesus. He is real.

"Faith without works is dead."

God has ordained that faith be acted upon. Faith lying dormant in your spirit is of little value. Faith must be used or released. 2 Corinthians 5:7. "We walk by faith and not by sight." Faith released by moving forward in the perfect will of God. So there must be a time of prayer and finding the will of God; then there is a steady moving forward in faith. This is not a step of knowledge. Peter had to step oyt by faith upon the water. Joshua's priests had to place their feet upon the water by faith before the Lord opened the Jordan River. Joshua 3:13.

"Wherefore criest thou unto me? Speak unto the children of Israel." There is a time to pray. There is a time to move out by faith. God would not open the Red Sea until Moses put his rod out over the sea in a positive act of faith.

"Go borrow thee vessels . . . thou shalt pour out . . ." Here is a woman who needed a miracle. Her husband had died. He left a huge debt for the family to pay. The boys were about to be placed in jail as slaves to work out the debt. The mother cried out to the man of God. "What shall I do?" He had the answer, but it required that she do something. She had to borrow pans from her neighbors. Then she had to pour out of the little oil that she had into the empty containers. As she obeyed, God met her; a miracle took place. All the vessels that she had borrowed were filled.

FEAR IS DESTROYED BY YOUR WILL

Romans 6:16 "Know ye not, that to whom ye yield yourselves to obey, his servants ye are to whom ye obey . . ."

Your will is king. Neither Satan nor God can work in your life without first gaining possession of your will. God has made it this way.

You are a free moral agent. Choose to yield to fears, failures, and frustrations; and they will be more than ready to dominate your life. Choose to yield to joy and deliverance in Jesus' name, and the Lord will be quick to move on your behalf. You have a decision to make.

I know a medical doctor who was having trouble with an infirmity in one of his patients. Medicine was not reaching the infirmity. After one month of working with her and her problem, he said to her: "Look, you are a child of God. You don't have to have this thing. Go home, and command it to leave you." She took his advice, and the infirmity left that very day.

Most of you fail to realize that you are making decisions daily that are setting the course for your life.

Many of these decisions are made when you are very little aware that you have made them. You have accepted failure and defeat as a way of life. You have considered it your lot. You have been yielding to circumstances for years. When problems arise, you automatically adjust for a long siege of struggle.

You have walked in the earthly so long that you consider the spirit approach, or the miracle approach, as the exception rather than the norm.

God is bringing you back to His Word. "If we

have faith . . . nothing shall be impossible." Matthew 17:20.

You are constantly making a decision. Your will determines whether you will be a failure or a success. Come above the natural, and live in the faith realm. "Whom ye yield yourselves servants to obey, his servants ye are . . ."

RIGHTEOUSNESS DESTROYS FEAR

Proverbs 1:33 "Whoso hearkeneth unto me shall dwell safely, and shall be quiet from fear of evil."

Isaiah 66:4 "I will bring their fears upon them because when I called, none did answer; when I spake, they did not hear: but they did evil before mine eyes . . ."

Isaiah 54:14 "In righteousness shalt thou be established: thou shalt be far from oppression; for thou shalt not fear: and from terror; for it shall not come near thee.

The seed bed for fear is wickedness. The results of wickedness are fear. A righteous life will eventually destroy all fears. "In righteousness shalt thou be established . . . thou shalt not fear."

Just recently I was dealing with a lad who had fears and many other problems. In counsel I was not able to reach him or find out the cause of his trouble. Upon yielding to the Holy Spirit, the Lord showed me that he was a homo-sexual. Prior to his becoming a homo-sexual, he had hated his father for many years. One sin paved the way for another. Finally, fears and mental confusion dominated him.

Fear may enter through circumstances that are, to a large part, out of your control. One girl that we ministered to had been molested by her father. Fear, frustration, and shock brought a complete mental break down. She gained partial deliverance by time and medical help. I cast the spirit of fear and frustration from her in Jesus' name. In this case, it was largely the sin of others that caused fear to enter. However, had this girl been taught correctly as a child, she could have forgiven her father and rejoiced her way to victory without having to go the mental break-down route.

Establish a spearhead of righteousness in any country, and the forces of wickedness can be driven back. An illustration of this is Gideon's 300 who destroyed a large army that came against Israel.

Begin now by drawing near to God in repentance. Even though you may be a victim of adverse circumstances, still you have yielded to fear and confusions. Choose righteousness today. As you draw near to God, He will draw near to you. James 4:8.

FEAR IS DESTROYED BY SEEKING GOD

Psalm 34:4 "I sought the Lord, and he heard me, and delivered me from all my fears."

Proverbs 2:4-5 "If thou seekest her as silver, and searchest for her as for hid treasures; Then thou shalt understand the fear of the Lord, and find the knowledge of God."

Psalm 107:9 "He satisfieth the longing soul, and filleth the hungry soul with goodness."

Isaiah 44:3 "I will pour water upon him that is thirsty, and floods upon dry ground."

"I sought the Lord and he heard me and delivered me from all my fears." There must be a hunger for God. It is exciting to get hungry for God. As you seek him, He does hear; and He does deliver you.

Pray this prayer with me. "Father, in Jesus' name, I submit myself to you. I am willing to be made willing. I desire to seek you with all my heart."

"He heard me and delivered me." This is God's way. He does hear. He does deliver from fear. Some of you have never really put God first. Others have not given God a chance. You seek Him with one thought or action and destroy your gain with the following thoughts or actions.

Confess with me: "I do seek the Lord today. He does hear me. He does deliver me." Now hold that confession. Regardless of symptoms to the contrary, keep a positive attitude.

"If you seek her as silver, and search for her as for hid treasure;" Here is the consistent determined search. If you lost a large treasure in the house or in the yard, you would search day and night until you found it.

I declare to you now, "There is victory from fear through Jesus Christ. Come to Him. Stay with Him. You will soon break through to the light."

"He satisfieth the longing soul, and filleth the hungry soul." Sometimes the Lord leaves us in the wilderness until our desire is stronger. True faith that delivers you from fears, etc. is born in a hungry, longing soul. It is the hungry soul that gets fed. Reach your hands up to receive from Jesus now.

Confess with me: "The Lord is pouring water upon my thirsty soul. He is pouring water upon my dry ground." Repeat this several times in an attitude of devotion to the Lord. Now just wave your hands to Jesus, and love Him. Let His spirit minister this truth into your spirit.

PERFECT LOVE DESTROYS FEAR

1 John 4:18 "There is no fear in love; but perfect love casteth out fear: because fear hath torment. He that feareth is not made perfect in love."

I John 4:12 "If we love one another, God dwelleth in us . . ."

Matthew 14:14 "Jesus . . . was moved with compassion toward them, and he healed their sick."

Perfect love is living in the very presence of God. Fear cannot live in the presence of God. If you love one another, God dwells in your midst. God takes over in full strength in the atmosphere of love.

Most problems come when you turn to fear, confusion, or even hate instead of love. Develop the love release for every problem. Determine to release love and joy rather than fear, hate, and self-pity.

Jesus moved in compassion and healed the sick. He moved with compassion and healed the leper. Mark 1:40-41. Love is God's nature. It is a fruit of the spirit. Hate is the devil's nature. Practice yielding to love.

The late William Branham, a prophet of God, demonstrated the power of love in breaking the power of fear.

One day he bumped a hornet nest with his lawn mower. They swarmed all over him. A wave of love and compassion swept over him for the hornets; then he commanded them to go back to their nest in Jesus' name. They lined up like soldiers and went back to their nest. Not one stung him.

On another occasion he moved with compassion and love for a demon possessed man who was threatening to kill him and destroy the service. Instead of moving in fear and calling for the police who were behind the maniac, he commanded the officers to let him alone with the man. The love of Jesus Christ flooded through him for the man. He looked upon him as some mother's son rather than an enemy who was making threats on his life. Then in a tremendous flow of compassion for the man and an authority from heaven, he commanded the demon to come out in Jesus' name. Instantly the demon came out. The man fell at his feet completely delivered.

Work on love. Satan cannot stand the love of God.

Slip your hand up to the Lord in complete surrender with love and devotion to Him, and make this confession: "Lord, I love you. I love my fellow man. I love this life you have given me. I love my family. I love my enemies." Now drink in His love as you worship Him for a few minutes. Learn to bathe in His love daily in a similar fashion.

If you find it impossible to love your enemies, then you must repent and forgive until you can.

FEAR IS DESTROYED AS JESUS ABIDES IN YOU AND YOU ABIDE IN HIM

Ephesians 3:17 "That Christ may dwell in your hearts by faith; that ye, being rooted and grounded in love."

John 14:23 "If a man love me, he will keep my words: and my Father will love him, and we will come unto him, and make our abode with him."

Jeremiah 42:10-11 "If ye will still abide in this land, then will I build you, and not pull you down, and I will plant you, and not pluck you up. Be not afraid of the king of Babylon, of whom ye are afraid."

"That Christ may dwell in your hearts by faith . . . rooted and grounded in love." Walking in Christ is a faith walk. Each new victory is taken by faith. As you refuse the outward feelings and appearances, and walk on in faith, the results are a Jesus take-over in your life. You actually move from one level of love and glory to a new level of love and glory. 2 Corinthians 3:18.

As you are dominated by Jesus, then love completely possesses you. It is completely impossible for fear to dwell in this atmosphere.

"He will keep my words and my Father will love him, and we will come unto him, and make our abode with him." Keeping His Words involves holy living. It is a life of faith. It is a life of the fruits of the spirit. Tender and peaceful spirits surround this life. Rest and joy make up the Christ life. As you practice this, then He does come and make His abode with you.

You are a product of your thoughts and actions from the day of birth. It is time for you to walk in Christ regardless of the pattern set by previous years of failure.

"If ye will still abide in this land, then will I build you." Make your choice. Determine to abide in the way of the Lord. Then He will come and build His life and victory in you.

The Lord allows you to be tested. Regardless of the time lapse between your struggle and your victory, hold fast. You will come through. Determine to abide in the way you have chosen, Christ Jesus.

"Be not afraid of the king of Babylon." Renounce the fear that is tormenting you. He is an enemy that has been destroyed by the Lord. He cannot stand in the presence of true faith.

God gives deliverance from the king of

Babylon. Many Christians are seeking refuge in Egypt from the king of Babylon. You must not turn to fleshly deliverance from your fears and problems.

Throughout the Word of God, God has admonished you not to fear the enemy.

Fear is a spirit out of hell that cannot be overcome with the natural.

Abiding in Jesus and walking in love, peace, and joy are the only defenses against the invasion of fear.

FEAR IS OVERCOME BY IDENTIFICATION WITH THE JESUS NATURE

> Romans 6:11 "Likewise reckon ye also yourselves to be dead indeed unto sin, but alive unto God through Jesus Christ our Lord."

> John 10:28 "I give unto them eternal life . . . (God life)"

> 2 Peter 1:4 "Whereby are given unto us exceeding great and precious promises: that by these ye might be partakers of his divine nature . . ."

A study of Romans 6:11 reveals that you are identified with Jesus in his death, burial, and resurrection. You share the very resurrection life of your Lord. You are now seated with Christ in the heavenlies. Ephesians 2:5-6. You have God life in you. John 10:28. (Eternal life means age lasting God-life in the original.) God himself abides in you. 2 Corinthians 6:16. Your body is a temple of the Holy Spirit. I Corinthians 6:19-20. You are being filled, as you walk in love, with the very fullness of God. Ephesians 3:19. Through His Word you become partakers of His divine nature. 2 Peter 1:4.

Stand tall in Jesus today. "Reckon yourselves to be dead indeed to sin, but alive unto God." You are dead to failure, dead to fear and defeat. You are now alive unto victory, joy, and the very resurrection life of Jesus Christ. Read Philippians 3:10. "That I may know Him, and the power of His resurrection . . ." Read Ephesians 1:19-20. "And what is the exceeding greatness of His power toward us who believe, according to the working of His mighty power, which He wrought in Christ, when He raised Him from the dead . . ."

Identify with your new life and nature. Christ is in you. His power is in you. His life is in you. Identify with this nature rather than the nature of Satan which is fear, failure, etc.

You are a new creature. 2 Corinthians 5:17. Old things have passed away. You no longer legally possess a fear or failure nature.

Your new and legal nature is the nature of Jesus Christ. You have the very life of God in you. You are partakers of His divine nature. You do not have a fear nature.

The fear nature belongs to the old life. It is of Satan. Stop identifying with what you were. Identify with the Jesus life in you.

Usually you are a victim of your own ignorance. Satan has taken advantage of you. He has given you a few symptoms of his nature and by this he has fully convinced you that you are full of fear and failure. Instead of defying him and rebelling against his lies, you have yielded to him and agreed with his symptoms. You have let symptoms be true and God a liar. Come alive to your new nature. "Let God be true and every man (symptom) a liar."

2 Corinthians 10:5. "Casting down imaginations, and every high thing (fear) that exalteth itself against the knowledge of God, and bringing into captivity every thought to the obedience of Christ."

Your new nature is fearlessness. The righteous are as bold as a lion. Cast down the lie called fear. Bring every thought captive to the Word of God. Confess daily: "I am as bold as a lion." "God is with me." "I am strong."

Stop identifying with the failure and fear nature. Identify with who you are in Christ. Reckon yourself to be dead to fear. Consider fear to be a past issue. It has no place in the nature of Christ. Consider yourself to be healed from fear and alive to Jesus Christ.

Any symptoms to the contrary are to be laughed at until they leave. They can only operate when you feed them with thoughts that agree with them.

As you work and go about your daily activities, constantly confess the fruits of the spirit and the life of Christ to be your legal nature. Laugh at the contrary thoughts which try to defy the Word of God.

When you are under pressure and are tempted to fall back into your old life pattern, begin to confess: "My legal nature is love, joy, peace, longsuffering, gentleness, goodness, faith, meekness, temperance." Don't worry about feelings. Begin to arouse your true and legal nature. Feed this nature. If you sin, repent. Put your sins under the blood. Come alive quickly to your forgiveness. Don't continue to grieve over your sin. That is Satanic. Rejoice your way back to joy.

FEAR IS OVERCOME BY DIRECT DELIVERANCE

> Mark 16:17 "These signs shall follow them that believe; In my name shall they cast out devils; they shall speak with new tongues."

> Acts 10:38 "God anointed Jesus of Nazareth with the Holy Ghost and with power; who went about doing good, and

healing all that were oppressed of the devil."

James 4:7 "Submit yourselves therefore to God. Resist the devil, and he will flee from you."

Fear is a spirit, and you can be delivered from it in many ways. In many cases, regardless of the severity of the problem, fear can be removed by direct deliverance.

The individual believer can deliver himself in Jesus' name; however, in some cases, the problem is so complex that believers need to come to the aid of one another.

I have discussed this at length in my book, *Setting the Captives Free.*

Basically, deliverance is based on genuine repentance and complete forgiveness of anyone that may be involved in either your present or past problems.

There is no set rule for deliverance that will cover every case. God has many approaches. When one is moving in the spirit, it is possible to have a different method in every case for deliverance. God is not bound by any pattern.

CHAPTER 4

FEAR YE NOT

FEAR NOT EVEN IN THE FACE OF MAJOR PROBLEMS

Psalm 23:4 "Yea, though I walk through the valley of the shadow of death, I will fear no evil: for thou art with me; thy rod and thy staff they comfort me."

Deuteronomy 3:22 "Ye shall not fear them: for the Lord your God, he shall fight for you."

Deuteronomy 20:3-4 "...Hear, O Israel, ye approach this day unto battle against your enemies: let not your hearts faint, fear not, and do not tremble, neither be ye terrified because of them; for the Lord your God is he that goeth with you, to fight for you against your enemies, to save you."

Deuteronomy 31:6 "Be strong and of a good courage, fear not, nor be afraid of them: for the Lord thy God, he it is that doth go with thee; he will not fail thee, nor forsake thee: fear not, neither be dismayed."

Hebrews 13:6 "So that we may boldly say, The Lord is my helper, and I will not fear what man shall do unto me."

"Though I walk through the valley of the shadow of death, I will fear no evil." Regardless of your problem, whether it be sickness, disaster, or apparent failure on every side, refuse to fear. Fear is a deadly enemy. The Lord is big enough to bring you victory if you refuse to fear.

"Ye shall not fear them: for the Lord your God, he shall fight for you." Whether your enemy be poverty, business problems, family problems, or personal shortcomings, you must train yourself never to yield to fear. Fear will destroy you quicker than the enemy on the outside. Fear admits that you are a failure. Fear falsely witnesses that there is no way through the darkness.

The only limitation you have is unbelief. Fear is unbelief. God can bring you through any crisis. "The Lord your God, he shall fight for you." Fear will stop the flow of faith that releases God. Faith will allow God to "whip" the enemy for you.

Deuteronomy 20:1. "When thou goest out to battle against thine enemies, and seest horses, and chariots, and a people more than thou, be not afraid of them: for the Lord thy God is with thee . . ." God did not remove the problem. He brought them through the problem. The only prerequisite that the Lord gave them for a great deliverance was always, "Hear, O Israel, ye approach this day unto battle against your enemies: let not your hearts faint, fear not, and do not tremble, neither be ye terrified because of them; for the Lord your God is he that goeth with you, to fight for you against your enemies, to save you."

I have a choice to yield to fear and go under or to victory and go over.

The will is king. Satan cannot gain victory over my will if I choose to yield to God and His nature. God's nature is not fear. God cannot work for you in the face of fear. Fear is a characteristic of the devil. Fear is merely saying, "Come here, Devil; I need you. Step aside, God; Satan and I will work this out." Whether you do this consciously or unconsciously, you are still doing it.

"Be strong and of a good courage, fear not . . . for the Lord thy God, He it is that goeth with thee, he will not fail thee nor forsake thee." You also have this same command in Ephesians 5:10. You are actually commanded by the Lord to take the "bull" by the horns and push the enemy back.

Jesus Christ is in you.

He knows no defeat.

You are more than conquerors through Him.

Satan is afraid of Jesus Christ. His power is at your disposal. Fear will not release Christ. It releases the enemy; therefore be strong; all things are yours. Be strong; you have been blessed with all spiritual blessings. Ephesians 1:3. Be strong; you are seated with Christ in heavenly places. Ephesians 2:5-6. Be strong; Christ dwells in you. Ephesians 3:17. Be strong; give no place to the devil. Ephesians 4:27. There is no cause to fear. You were not made to fear. You were created into Christ Jesus to make the devil fear and tremble.

"We may boldly say, the Lord is my helper, I will not fear . . ." God said it so that you may boldly say it. Say it now: "God is with me. He is my helper. He is my deliverer. He is my healer. He is my finances. He brings me through today. He is with me. I am strong. I live victoriously today over all the power of the enemy." Now keep on saying it during the day. The Word of God is written so that you may boldly declare the power of Christ in you, today.

FEAR NOT, FOR GOD IS THY SALVATION

Genesis 15:1 "After these things the Word of the Lord came unto Abraham in a vision, saying, Fear not, Abram: I am thy shield, and thy exceeding great reward."

Abraham was childless. He was deeply concerned about having no son. His own concern was expressed as follows. "I go childless." Circumstances were against Abraham. Everything looked dark. How could God bless him and make his seed to multiply as the stars of heaven?

Many of you get in the same frame of mind as you approach God for your answers. You look to your natural abilities. You present to God your problems rather than your faith.

Genesis 15:4. ". . . He that shall come forth out of thine own bowels shall be thine heir." God has the answer to your seemingly impossible problem. Refuse to yield to fear. Out of your weakness God will shew himself strong. Deliverance did not come by Abraham's own scheming and planning.

Abraham continued to fear and to work it out on his own. He tried it with Hagar hoping that her child might be the heir, but the Lord rejected this work of the flesh.

Too often, the Christian operates in Hagar

type religion. This is the do it yourself way. Many of our churches and denominations are in the Hagar way, today.

Thank the Lord, Abraham finally learned to relax and trust the Lord. Romans 4:19-21. "Being not weak in faith, he considered not his own body now dead, when he was about an hundred years old, neither yet the deadness of Sarah's womb: He staggered not at the promise of God through unbelief; but was strong in faith, giving glory to God; Being fully persuaded that, what he had promised, he was able also to perform."

Fear departed and faith took hold of another miracle. What is your problem, today? Stop the Hagar battle. Get into your rest in the Lord. Enjoy your heavenly Father. Watch as He makes havoc of the enemy. He is waiting.

When Abraham took his mind off the circumstances, he became a victor. He took his mind off his old age as well as that of his wife. He took his mind off the fact that even when Sarah was young, she could not bear children. He put this mind on the promise and declared himself a father of Isaac. Right then was when his miracle was born. Faith first releases in the spirit realm.

FEAR NOT, FOR GOD IS THY PROTECTION

Psalm 46:1-3 "God is our refuge and strength, a very present help in trouble. Therefore will not we fear, though the earth be removed, and though the mountains be carried into the midst of the sea; Though the waters thereof roar and be troubled, though the mountains shake with swelling thereof."

Make a bold positive confession now: "God is my refuge. God is my strength. God is now my help. He is delivering me from this present problem."

Run to the 91st Psalm. Confess: "I am dwelling in the secret place of the most high. The Lord is my refuge. I will not be afraid. A thousand shall fall at my side, and ten thousand at my right hand; but it shall not come nigh to me. No evil shall befall me. No plague shall come nigh my dwelling. He will give his angels charge over me to keep me in all of my ways. They will bear me up in their hands, lest I dash my feet against a stone. I will tread on the lion and the adder: the young lion and the dragon I will trample under my feet."

Repeat this over several times a day. Insert your children's names instead of yours. Confess it. Believe it. Stand on it. Fear will have to go.

FEAR NOT; GOD WILL HELP YOU

Isaiah 41:10, 13-15 "Fear thou not; for I am with thee: be not dismayed; for I am thy God: I will strengthen thee; yea, I will help thee; yea, I will uphold thee with the right hand of my righteousness. For I the Lord thy God will hold thy right hand, saying unto thee, Fear not; I will help thee. Fear not, thou worm Jacob, and ye men of Israel; I will help thee, saith the Lord, and thy redeemer, the Holy One of Israel. Behold, I will make thee a new sharp threshing instrument having teeth: thou shalt thresh the mountains, and beat them small, and shalt make the hills as chaff."

Regardless of the circumstances, God always admonished His children to fear not. He knew that He could carry them through if they would not yield to fear. Israel indeed had problems. Nations were warring against her. Isaiah 41:12. All hope was gone. God always had the answer. God never has run short of power to deliver; He has run short on believers, however.

To be sure, they had no back bone. They were like worms with no strength. They were defenseless. Then the Lord came through. "Fear not, you worm, I will help thee . . . I will make thee a new sharp threshing instrument having teeth: Thou shalt thresh the mountains."

God has a sense of humor. Fear not, you worm, is His command. I will help thee. I will make a bulldozer out of you, you worm. I will put a ripper blade on your tail and a bulldozer on your nose. You will surely thresh the mountain. Your problems will turn to fine powder, and the wind will blow them away.

Rejoice, today. You are God's super-child in Jesus' name. You are His mountain mover. You are His devil chaser.

Yes, God does have a sense of humor. A worm has no strength. He has a terrible inferiority complex. People step on worms. He is a nothing. He is a nobody. No one brings out the red carpet for him. He is something to be trodden upon. God encourages the little fellow, however, by saying to him, "All I need is your confidence. Just don't be afraid. You and I can destroy any mountain or problem. Just relax. I am about to make a super-victor out of you. Your problem has become my opportunity to work the enemy over publicly."

Get excited, little worm. God is about to perform the impossible. Little you and big God are going to handle your mountain. It won't take a man-made program. It won't take being on the inside of a clique or even knowing the right people. It will just take the Lord. You have the key. Fear thou not!

FEAR NOT; GOD WILL DELIVER YOU

Exodus 14:13-14 "Moses said unto the people, Fear ye not, stand still, and see the salvation of the Lord, which he will shew to you today: for the Egyptians whom ye have seen today, ye shall see them again no more forever. The Lord shall fight for you, and ye shall hold your peace."

"Pharoah drew nigh, the children of Israel lifted up their eyes, and, behold, the Egyptians marched after them; and they were sore afraid . . ." Exodus 14:10.

Is the enemy coming down the hill after you? Does it seem as though you have been hemmed in on every side? Relax. Deliberately yield to joy and trust.

The children of Israel made the mistake that many of you so often have made. They lifted up their eyes and beheld their problem.

Your solution is not in looking to your problem. Your victory is in looking to Jesus. Hebrews 12:2.

Your victory is in bringing every thought captive to Christ. 2 Corinthians 10:5.

Looking to your problem creates more problem. Looking to the promise of God and confessing what God says brings victory.

Psalm 27:1-3 "The Lord is my light and

> my salvation; whom shall I fear? The Lord is the strength of my life; of whom shall I be afraid? When the wicked, even mine enemies and my foes came upon me to eat up my flesh, they stumbled and fell. Though an host should encamp against me, my heart shall not fear; though war should rise against me, in this will I be confident."

You, too, can have a strong, bold confession like this. Declare right now: "God is my light and my deliverance. I am not afraid. The Lord is my business strength. He is my family strength. He is my spiritual strength. I will not fear."

Now think on this. Meditate on this truth until it becomes a part of your spirit life. Let the Word of God remold your response to problems.

The Psalmist was so conditioned by the Word of God that he refused to go by his circumstances. Even though the enemy would camp on his door step, he refused to yield to fear. Even though war of all sorts broke out, he would not allow his heart to fear. He said, "I will be confident." Let problems be a challenge to you. Let them become your opportunity for growth into greater victories.

FEAR NOT; GOD HAS ALREADY GIVEN YOU THE VICTORY

> Joshua 8:1 "The Lord said unto Joshua, Fear not, neither be thou dismayed: take all the people of war with thee, and arise, go up to Ai: see, I have given unto thy hand the king of Ai, and his people, and his city, and his land."

In Joshua's mind the battle had not been won. God looked at it differently. He saw the end. So he said, "Do not fear. The battle has already been won."

God always cried out to his children in the face of all odds: "Fear not, I am with thee. I will help thee." Let this be your response to all of your problems.

Confess with me: "I will not fear today. I am strong. The Lord is with me. He is helping me today."

Jesus won the victory for us. Colossians 2:15. He spoiled principalities and powers. He made a show of them publicly. We are now in Jesus. His victories are our victories. Nothing can stop your victory from moving on to greater victories and greater heights in God if you refuse fear.

Notice that even though the battle was won, Joshua still had to go forth into the battle; but he went with the Lord. God took him through. You and I have to do some things by faith. That is, we find the mind of the Lord; then we walk out against the enemy with confidence.

Joshua did not have the mind of the Lord the first time they went against Ai, and he lost the battle. It was when they dealt with sin in the camp that they found the mind of God, again. Then they easily defeated Ai.

FEAR NOT; GOD DELIGHTS TO GIVE YOU THE KINGDOM, TODAY

> Luke 12:31-32 "Seek ye the kingdom of God; and all these things shall be added to you. Fear not, little flock; for it is your Father's good pleasure to give you the kingdom.

> Romans 8:15 "For ye have not received the spirit of bondage again to fear; but ye have received the Spirit of adoption whereby we cry, Abba, Father."

"Seek ye first the kingdom of God." This is a matter of choice on your part. It is a matter of yielding to the Lord rather than the enemy. It is hard to get victory over fear unless you seek first the Lord Jesus Christ. Jesus must be the king in your life. Your whole heart and being must move in surrender to His will.

"Fear not little flock." How the Lord

repeats this over and over to you. What is He saying to you? He is saying, "Look, I am with you. Believe it. I am your deliverance. Believe it. I am your provisions. Believe it. Just put me first; I'll take care of everything else."

"It is your Father's good pleasure to give you the kingdom." It is the Lord's good pleasure to bless you. It gives the Lord joy to bless you with anything your heart desires. However, He can not do it if you are deliberately wandering off into the devil's territory. So you absolutely must seek first the kingdom of God. He awaits your love and surrender. He has nothing to withhold from you. "No good thing will He withhold from those who walk uprightly." He desires to "Open unto you His good treasures."

May you come alive to His love, today.

"Ye have not received the spirit of bondage again to fear; but ye have received the Spirit of adoption whereby we cry, Abba, Father." Do not question your position before the Father. He is your Father. You are His son. He loves you.

Do not approach Him on the basis of your perfection, either. Approach as an adopted son. Come by the way of the blood of Jesus. Ask for forgiveness. Walk in it. Believe in your forgiveness. Daily, you will then be able to build a more Christ like walk!

Now confess with me: "I am not under the bondage of fear. I am an adopted son. God is my own personal Father God. I am His favorite son." Now repeat this confession. Close your eyes and meditate on this a few minutes. Let it go deep into your spirit. Now repeat it over and over, silently.

GOD HAS NOT GIVEN YOU FEAR

> **2 Timothy 1:7 "For God hath not given us the spirit of fear . . ."**

It is clear by this that fear is a product of the devil. Fear to witness for Jesus is certainly the enemy. Fear to go into a room alone is of the enemy. (Do not get this confused with warnings from The Holy Spirit about going certain places, etc.) Fear to drive or ride in a car after having had an accident is of the enemy. Fear of man is of the enemy.

If you are tormented with fears and frustrations in life, let it be settled once and for all. This is a work of Satan. It is not God's will for your life. You are a child of God. Fear has nothing to do with your legal nature. Your legal nature is joy and peace. Satan has invaded. Get him out today.

YOUR BATTLE IS GOD'S BATTLE

> **2 Chronicles 20:17 "Ye shall not need to fight in this battle: set yourselves, stand ye still, and see the salvation of the Lord**

with you . . . Fear not, nor be dismayed; tomorrow go out against them; for the Lord will be with you."

Strivings in the flesh are of little value in the kingdom walk. This does not encourage idleness. You will be very active, but it does do away with fleshly motives and activities.

"Set yourselves." Be determined to believe God. Be firm against contrary forces and situations. Learn to laugh at your problems.

"Stand still." There is a rest in the Lord. Enjoy it, today. Be anxious in nothing, but in everything by prayer and supplication with thanksgiving is Paul's word for us. So we get still by prayer and praise. God will work it out. Too often, we go ahead on our own. If you have prayed about it; if you have praised about it; then wait for the signal from the Holy Spirit. Move forward softly. Do not be determined to do your thing. Commit it all to Jesus. Be willing to be made willing. Say with me now: "Thy will be done. I submit to the Holy Ghost, today. I am willing for you to work out your perfect will in me, today."

Now you are about to "See the Salvation of the Lord." One swipe of His big hand against your enemy puts him out of commission.

Be determined that you are going to follow this simple rule. Proverbs 12:24. "The hand of the diligent shall bear rule . . ." Rule over your problem in Jesus' name, today. All of the resources of heaven are behind you. Christ is in you. He stands ready to reveal to you His way in every crisis.

Set your spiritual "Jaw," and determine to rule over your situation, now.

FEAR YE NOT TO TAKE THE LAND, TODAY

> Deuteronomy 1:21 "The Lord thy God hath set the land before thee; go up and possess it, as the Lord God of thy fathers hath said unto thee; fear not, neither be discouraged."

> Deuteronomy 3:22 "Ye shall not fear them: for the Lord your God he shall fight for you."

The land of Canaan was before them. The command was: "Go and possess . . . fear not, neither be discouraged." Their response was fear, worry, and unbelief. For this error they spent 40 years in the wilderness. God provided his second best for them in the wilderness. It was just a day by day existence. Many have that type of faith, today. They believe God for just bare necessities. In the land of

Canaan they found food on the shelves. They found an abundance. There was no want of anything in the earth. Jesus came to give us an abundance. Read John 10:10. Fear not. Believe God, today, for an abundance of everything good.

Fear and unbelief will keep you from moving into Canaan's land. It will keep you from moving into the fullness of Canaan's provisions once you have crossed over the Jordan.

Fear will keep you from moving forward in your ministry.

Fear will keep you in bondage to sickness, failure, and poverty.

"I the Lord have set the land before thee." God has set the kingdom before you. He has given it unto you. You are now in the kingdom. The kingdom of God is in you. Hesitate no longer in the wilderness of fear and unbelief.

Often, you send out the fearful spies to spy out the land. Then you are prone to believe the carnal report rather than the faith report.

The things of the kingdom do not always make sense to the natural man. Ten of the twelve spies sent to spy out the Promised Land returned with a fearful and negative report, and only two returned with a victory report. They went by the carnal report. This drew the wrath of God upon them, and they were forced to stay in the wilderness for forty years until all the flesh died away. You must learn with Paul to keep the flesh under. I Corinthians 9:27.

Fearful and negative responses of the fleshly mind will bring bondage to God's children. This must be thrown off. The body of Christ is being released in this world. You cannot operate in the religion of flesh any longer. You cannot afford to spend another forty years in the wilderness.

Arise now, and take your land of deliverance.

Arise now, and take your God-given land of abundance from the clutches of Satan.

Arise now, and take your God-given healing from the hands of the devil.

Arise now, and take your God-given joy from the spirits of demonic depression.

Let the peace of Christ rule in your hearts rather than strife, turmoil, and fear.

Refuse to sit in the shadow of the Promised Land. Come over into Canaan, today. Arise, today, and do exploits in Jesus' name. You are reigning, today. You are taking the land, today. You are prospering, today. You have favor with God and man, today. Declare it! Believe it! Hold on to it! Now, get excited!

FEAR NOT THE NATURE OF YOUR PROBLEM OR THE SIZE

Deuteronomy 20:3-4 "Ye approach this day unto battle against your enemies: let

not your hearts faint, fear not, and do not tremble, neither be ye terrified because of them. For the Lord your God is he that goeth with you, to fight for you against your enemies to save you."

Today, you will approach unto battle against the devil and his forces. Refuse to be faint hearted and fearful. Do not tremble. Do not be terrified at the sight of the enemy. Remember the Lord is going before you to fight for you. He will save you from your enemies, today.

Satan tries to throw fear into you. He tries to get your mind on your problem, etc. Get your mind on the Word. Relax. Laugh at the situation. The Lord will fight for you, today.

Remember fear will stop the flow of God to you, today. Joy and trust will release the flow. Begin now to release joy, faith, and hope.

Deuteronomy 31:6 "Be strong and of a good courage; fear not, nor be afraid of them: for the Lord thy God, He it is that doth go with thee; He will not fail thee, nor forsake thee."

Stand up, today. Say it with me: "I am strong, today. I am strong in Jesus' strength. I am very courageous, today. I am not afraid. God is with me, today. The Lord goeth with me, today. He will not fail me. I cannot fail."

Now hold this confession. Keep referring to this. Meditate on it. Let God's Word replace fearful thoughts and attitudes.

> Isaiah 35:3-4 "Strengthen ye the weak hands and confirm the feeble knees. Say to them that are of a fearful heart, Be strong; fear not; behold your God will come with vengeance . . . he will come and save you."

The pressure is on your back to get out of your situation. You strengthen the weak hands. You confirm the feeble knees. This may be your problem, or it may be another's. You have the responsibility of taking what the Lord has provided for you. Take your health. Take your financial blessing. Take your ministry. Jesus has given it to you. You strengthen the feeble knees. You strengthen your weak hands. You are God's overcomer. Get up, today, and get on with the power that was given you through Christ. You are a joint heir with Him. Take this power by faith. It is yours.

You say to them that are of a fearful heart, "Be strong, fear not . . . God will come and save you." Speak positive words of victory to yourself and to others. This releases the Lord's power through us.

Say it with me now: "I am strong. I do not

have a fearful heart. I have an abundance spiritually, physically, mentally, and financially. I am a king, today, through Jesus Christ. Get out of my way, devil. I am coming alive, today. I am a son of God, born to reign. Hallelujah."

> 2 Kings 6:15-16 "And when the servant of the man of God was risen early, and gone forth, behold, an host compassed the city both with horses and chariots. And his servants said unto him, Alas, My master! how shall we do? And he answered, Fear not: for they that be with us are more than they that be with them."

Spiritual eyes do not look at the host that compasses on every side. They do not look at the problem before them. They look into the mind of God and see the answer. The man of God could see the angels of God encamped around about. He could see that God was present in greater force than the enemy.

This is what God has been telling you in all these verses. In each case He has said, "Now you are coming against your enemy. He looks very big to the natural eye, but do not fear the outward appearance, for I am with you, and that makes you a majority in any circumstance. Just don't fear."

FEAR NOT BECAUSE OF YOUR SHORT-COMINGS

I Kings 17:13 "Fear not: go and do as thou hast said; but make me thereof a little cake first, and bring it unto me, and after make for thee and for thy son."

These are the words of the Lord to a little widow lady who was practically out of food. She was about to make her last loaf of bread for herself and her son. Famine was in the land. She anticipated death. The prophet said, "Fear not." This is the first step toward victory. Refuse to fear. God is present to set you free. To release herself from the grips of fear, she had to take a bold step of faith. She had to obey the Word and make the prophet a little cake first with the understanding that as she gave to the man of God, God would meet her and give her a miracle.

If you will read the verses that follow this, you will find that she did just this. She made a cake for the prophet; then she returned and made one for herself and her son. In fact, God gave them such a miracle that she, her house, and the prophet lived many days on the barrel of meal which wasted not; neither did the cruse of oil fail until the Lord sent rain upon the earth.

This little widow woman found the secret.

Instead of yielding to fear and selfishness which are demonic, she yielded to obedience and trust which are Godly. As she yielded to Godly attitudes, fear was swallowed up, and God met her needs.

I have been in milder situations myself. At times I have gone to service with only five dollars in my pocket and no money coming in to meet our daily needs. The spirit of God has spoken many times to me that I should give. My first response was usually one of fear. I would say, "Lord, I have more needs than this preacher does. I need this money myself." Then the Lord would say, "Give and I will make men give unto you." He has never, never failed that promise, yet.

Some time ago the Lord told me to pay off a five hundred dollar debt for a preacher. I didn't want to do it, but I knew that obedience was the secret to miracle power. After I paid off the debt, God moved on a person to give me one thousand dollars. Hallelujah! The Lord is bigger than any problem.

FEAR NOT WHEN IT SEEMS THAT THE PROBLEM IS FAR TOO GREAT TO BEAR

> Isaiah 43:1-2 "Fear not: for I have redeemed thee, I have called thee by thy name, Thou art mine, When thou passeth thru the waters, I will be with thee, and through the rivers, they shall not over-

flow thee; when thou walkest thru the fire, thou shalt not be burned."

"I have redeemed thee." God loves you. He has a special interest in you. He sent His Son to die for you. You are His! Come alive! You are someone very special!

"I have called thee by thy name." Yes, God knows you personally. John 10:3. ". . . He calleth his own sheep by name." You have your own personal Jesus Christ and Father God. He knows you. He knows all about you. He is with you every moment. He cares. Trust Him, today, to bring you through. Do not fear.

"Thou art mine." He is jealous over you. He has an interest in you. You are His property. He wants you to have the victory over the devil more than you do. He has an investment in you. As you walk in the victory, then He gets a return. You let your light shine before men, and the heavenly Father is glorified. Yes, He desires your victory. He desires that you overcome the devil. You are His. Lean on His shoulder today. Place your head on His bosom, today. Just snuggle up to Him and dare the enemy to touch you. Now relax in His presence, and let the devil "snort" all he wants to. He is a phony and a fake.

"When thou passeth thru the waters, I will be with thee." Troubled waters do not separate you from the Lord. They bring you closer to Him. Rejoice when you have troubled waters. This draws you closer to Jesus. He abides in the praise of His people and pushes the troubled waters away.

Close your eyes and repeat over and over, "God is with me now. He is with me now. He delivers me now." Now get very quiet and worship and love Him in your spirit. This is meditating the Word into your spirit. As you read Psalm 1, you will find that the one who meditates on God's Word becomes like a tree planted by the waters. His leaf will not wither. He will bring forth fruit in season. Whatever he does will be prosperous.

There are times when you shall "walk thru the fire", but you will not be burned. Pressures may come. Problems may come. Sometimes the Lord allows these to perfect you in the Way. Psalm 119:71. "It is good for me that I have been afflicted; that I might learn thy statutes." If they do come, rejoice; but do not fear.

Sometime ago I purchased a used trailer and rebuilt it. We had an investment of four thousand dollars in it. On our first trip, due to a faulty oven valve, we blew it up. I was standing before the oven when I lit the match. My wife was standing nearby. When it blew up, it knocked the closet door off its hinges and hit my wife on the head. It only singed my hair a little. I could not figure how the door fell off or how the bed turned over in the bed room. My first immediate response was, Oh, me, there goes four thousand dollars. Then almost immediately I began to rejoice and thank the Lord. As it turned out, we found, later, that the damage was fairly minor. We were able to jack the side of the trailer back into shape, reset the cabinets and bed which were blown loose from the wall, replace all the window hardware which ruptured in the explosion, and replace some clothes that burned without too much expense.

The miracle is this. We were in the very middle of this, and we did not get burned.

DO NOT BE AFRAID ALONE AT NIGHT

> Proverbs 3:24-26 "When thou liest down, thou shalt not be afraid, yea, thou shalt lie down, and thy sleep shall be sweet. Be not afraid of sudden fear, neither of the desolation of the wicked, when it cometh. For the Lord shall be thy confidence, and shall keep thy foot from being taken."

Make this bold confession: "In Jesus' name I shall not be afraid, tonight." Stop identifying with fear. Identify with your new and legal nature.

Confess with me: "I am as bold as a lion." Read Proverbs 28:1.

"You shall lie down, and thy sleep shall be sweet." Anticipate this. Believe this. Look forward to it. Confess it aloud to yourself and others.

Some tell me of visitations by evil spirits in the night. They ask me how to stop this.

One way is get your deliverance. Close up the gaps. Repent if there is known sin. Draw nigh to God, and He will draw nigh unto you. Resist the devil, and he will flee from you. Plead the blood over your house and especially the bed room. Get others to come in and help you do this. One will chase a thousand, but two can put ten thousand to flight.

Keep confessing over and over: "I will lie down, and my sleep shall be sweet. I will have peace tonight. Satan cannot visit me."

Keep this up daily until all signs of these visitations cease. Then continue it from time to time.

If you still have trouble, then seek further help. Perhaps you are overlooking something in your own life and need further help.

> Psalm 91:4-5, 10 "He shall cover thee with his feathers, and under his wings shalt thou trust: his truth shall be thy shield and buckler. Thou shalt not be afraid for the terror by night; nor for the arrow that flieth by day. There shall no evil befall thee, neither shall any plague come nigh thy dwelling."

"He shall cover thee." Let this be your confession rather than fear.

"Under His wings shalt thou trust." Rest in your position in Christ. You are snuggled away under His wing right now. You are resting in His presence. No harm shall come to you.

One lady called and said her husband had threatened her life. She felt that she could not keep running and hiding from him so I prayed the scriptures listed here in Psalm 91. We made them very personal to her. That very night the husband came and broke into the house; however, he could not touch her. He turned and left the house without touching her or the children or anything in the house except where he broke in. Satan was bound by the truth. She operated in the truth. The truth set her free.

"Thou shalt not be afraid for the terror by night." Confess: "I will fear no evil, today or tonight. My family shall fear no evil. God is with us."

"Thou shalt not be afraid . . . of the arrow that flieth by day." Repeat with me: "I will fear no problems, today. I will not fear failure, today. I will not fear insecurity, today. My family shall not fear, today. The Lord is with us." Now take time to repeat this several times. Meditate on this.

"No evil shall befall thee." Make this personal. Stop treating God's Word as if it were a history book. Apply it to your life as well as the life of your family. Make a bold confession: "No evil shall befall me, today. No evil shall befall my loved ones. God is with us." Maintain a tender and humble spirit before the Lord as you obey His Word.

"No plague shall come nigh thy dwelling." What a precious verse and promise the Lord has given you. No plague shall come nigh your home, today. Rely on this. Confess it. Expect it to happen.

When my son was in Viet Nam, my wife and I confessed the 91st Psalm daily on his behalf. We would apply it to him personally as I have been doing in these verses. God honored our confession as well as that of other members of our family who were also praying for him along with many, many friends.

He was flying a helicopter over enemy fire almost constantly, yet God kept him and gave him one of the best safety records of anyone in his outfit. Hallelujah. All praise to the Lord Jesus Christ.

"His truth shall be thy shield." At times my son would feel a shield over and around him as he would fly in the midst of enemy fire. Sometimes everyone else would turn and leave the scene of action for one reason or another, leaving him flying alone. He said, "I just kept on going. It felt as though there was a shield around me." There really was one, too. Praise to the Lord.

BOOKS BY BOB BUESS

King David and I. 1.95
High Flight. 1.95
Implanted Word. 1.95
The Race Horse. 1.25
Discipleship Pro and Con. 1.95
The Pendulum Swings. 1.95
The Laws of the Spirit. 1.50
Setting the Captives Free. 1.50
Deliverance From the
Bondage of Fear. 1.50
Favor, the Road to Success. 1.25
You Can Receive
the Holy Ghost Today. 1.50
Confession Pack
(Scripture cards). 1.00

All 12 of the above for $15.00 including postage. This is a $20.00 value for only $15.00!

When ordering up to 3 books include 60¢ postage.

Add 20¢ for each additional 3 books or fraction thereof.

Texas residents please include 4% sales tax unless you are qualified for tax exemption.

In orders of 30 books or more, you may deduct 35%.

Please add postage and sales tax on discounted total, if applicable.

Bookstores and jobbers receive other discounts.

No discounts when ordering at the special set prices.